Family Lineage of Permenter Morgan and Descendants of Rutherford and Buncombe, North Carolina

(2018 Edition)

includes sources and name index

Researched and Compiled by
Dawn D. Boyer, Ph.D.

COPYRIGHT 2018©

Published by:	Dawn D. Boyer, B.F.A., M.F.A. Ph.D. D. Boyer Consulting, Sandston, VA 23150 www.DBoyerConsulting.com / Dawn.Boyer@dboyerconsulting.com
Book Copyright:	2018© by Dawn D. Boyer, Ph.D.
ISBN Numbers:	ISBN-13: 978-1987738971 ISBN-10: 1987738977 CSID# 8343011

No part of this book or images – black and white, or other renditions of images, are to be posted to any social media, Internet, and/or other digital media or platforms without prior written permission of the copyright owner. You are supporting writers and allowing the author to continue to publish books for readers to continue to enjoy.

Disclaimer: The author has attempted to gather as much of the facts and information to the utmost complete and truthfulness for the compilation of this book from bona fide sources, Internet sources, printed material in currently circulating and non-circulating library sources, newspaper articles, personal interviews, and the memories of families involved in this surname lineage. The author cannot and will not offer any guarantees that each and every bit of information is 100% accurate or factually true. The reader should keep this in mind and understand that if any information that may have been included (or left out) is not correct, it is not the fault of the author. Several bodies of research were interpretations of the same or original documents and errors may have occurred as transcribed. Some material was pulled from Internet sources with no proof or source guidance, but facts offered 'seemed to fit' or match other known and provable facts. The author welcomes all corrections and additions to the current material in anticipation of an extended and updated lineage book in the future. Anyone with more data to contribute to a future, updated, and corrected version of this genealogy project are encouraged to send materials to the author via the email noted.

Any personal information (e.g., birthdates, addresses, personal insights) of living persons are obtained from publicly available records; the author assumes data has been provided with permission and has been made publicly available by that living person; the author is not legally responsible for any identify theft or any complications arising from this publicly available data.

Author's Business Website	http://www.DBoyerConsulting.com
Amazon Author Page:	https://www.amazon.com/author/dawnboyer
Review Author's Books:	http://www.shelfari.com/DawnDeniseBoyer
Facebook Artist's Page:	http://www.Facebook.com/DawnBoyerArtist
Facebook Author's Page:	http://www.facebook.com/DawnBoyerAuthor
Facebook Business Page:	http://www.Facebook.com/DBoyerConsulting
Facebook Coloring Group Pages:	https://www.facebook.com/groups/ColoringColoringColoring/ https://www.facebook.com/groups/ColoringPagesByDawnBoyer/
Google+ Business Page:	https://plus.google.com/112802498128568560150/about?hl=en
LinkedIn	http://www.linkedin.com/in/DawnBoyer
Twitter:	http://www.Twitter.com/Dawn_Boyer
Pinterest:	https://www.pinterest.com/dawnboyer/coloring-books-for-adults/

Find the Author's Artwork, Coloring Page Sample Packs, and
Fine Art Illustrations for Sale on these Online Stores

Etsy:	https://www.etsy.com/people/DawnDBoyer
Fine Art America	http://fineartamerica.com/profiles/dawn-boyer.html

Introduction

The family lineage published in this book (and the author's other genealogy lineage books) are compilations resulting from 20+ years of transcriptions from multiple resources, personal family interviews, family letters and bibles. ancestor's compilations, county history books, online and Internet genealogy groups, and other library database or book resources. The author spent over two decades compiling the data points in this publication for this specific family surname, as well as hundreds of other surnames that interlinked and intertwined to her own family and ancestry surnames. Do enjoy the fruits of the research to expand the readers knowledge of this family surname.

Where specific birth dates were missing, the author entered a broad range for the birth date triangulated between the parent's potential birth and death dates, the mother's age for child-bearing, and the potential date for person's naturally and physicaly being able to have children.

As noted on the copyright page, any data errors may have resulted from human transcription mistakes, the original data having errors or omissions even though the transcription was true, or even 'software burps' or data entry errors (e.g., a husband may have been entered as a spouse twice, thus shows up as a duplicate). The author suggests genealogy researchers take the data information in this book and use it 'with a grain of salt' as a baseline to further research on their own to confirm all the data in this publication against their own information.

1 Permenter MORGAN[1,2]

Birth: BET 1730 AND 1765[2]

Spouse: **Gracie JONES** (BET 1730 AND 1765-)
Birth: BET 1730 AND 1765[2]

1 Child...
      James Squire (27 Oct 1780-25 Oct 1854)

1.1 James Squire MORGAN[1,2]

Birth: 27 Oct 1780, Rutherford County, North Carolina[2]
Burial: Miller Cemetery, Buncombe County, North Carolina.[2]
Death: 25 Oct 1854, Buncombe County, North Carolina[2]
Father: **Permenter MORGAN** (BET 1730 AND 1765-)
Mother: **Gracie JONES** (BET 1730 AND 1765-)

James Morgan was listed in the 1810 census in Rutherford County, North Carolina and on 1820, 1830, 1840, and 1850 in Buncombe County, North Carolina.
James and Margaret (Peggy) Morgan had 14 children.

Spouse: **Margaret (Peggy) GRANT** (abt 1788-10 Sep 1845)
Birth: abt 1788, Rutherford County, North Carolina[2]
Death: 10 Sep 1845, Buncombe County, North Carolina[2]
Father: **Alexander GRANT** (BET 1755 AND 1757-BET APR 1805 AND JUL 1806)
Mother: **Susanna MORRIS** (BET 1765 AND 1768-abt Mar 1825)

Proven daughter of Alexander Grant by a Rutherford County, North Carolina deed dated January 31, 1826 (Book 36, page 20).

Marriage: 17 Dec 1802, Rutherford County, North Carolina[3]

14 Children...
      Susan Tabitha (abt 1804-BET 1839 AND 1840)
      Permenter D. Sr. (26 Jun 1806-29 Jan 1865)

Mary (Polly) (abt 1808-27 Jan 1877)
Morris Grant Sr. (BET 1809 AND 1810-)
Jones H. (4 Sep 1812-16 Jul 1854)
Margaret (BET 1813 AND 1814-abt 1870)
Lewis R. (BET 1816 AND 1817-aft 1880)
Martha (abt 1817-)
James (1 Feb 1820-1 Apr 1891)
Millie (abt 1822-)
Elijah (9 Aug 1824-27 Oct 1879)
Stephen A. Sr. (BET 1827 AND 1828-aft 1880)
John Gano (BET 1828 AND 1829-aft 1880)
Martha (BET 1839 AND 1840-)

1.1.1 Susan Tabitha MORGAN[1,2]

Birth:	abt 1804, Rutherford County, North Carolina[2]
Death:	BET 1839 AND 1840, Buncombe County, North Carolina[2]
Father:	**James Squire MORGAN** (27 Oct 1780-25 Oct 1854)
Mother:	**Margaret (Peggy) GRANT** (abt 1788-10 Sep 1845)

Spouse:	**Uriah WARREN Sr.** (BET 1809 AND 1810-aft 1880)
Birth:	BET 1809 AND 1810, Buncombe County, North Carolina[2]
Death:	aft 1880, Buncombe County, North Carolina[2]
Father:	**James WARREN** (BET 1750 AND 1785-)
Mother:	**WIFE OF JAMES WARREN** (BET 1750 AND 1785-)
Marriage:	BET 1820 AND 1829, Bun[3]

5 Children...
    Mary S. (BET 1828 AND 1829-)
    Milly L. (BET 1834 AND 1835-)
    Josiah (BET 1834 AND 1835-)
    Uriah Jr. (BET 1836 AND 1837-)
    William H. (BET 1838 AND 1839-)

1.1.1.1 Mary S. WARREN[1,2]

Birth:	BET 1828 AND 1829, Buncombe County, North Carolina[2]
Father:	**Uriah WARREN Sr.** (BET 1809 AND 1810-aft 1880)
Mother:	**Susan Tabitha MORGAN** (abt 1804-BET 1839 AND 1840)

1.1.1.2 Milly L. WARREN[1,2]

Birth:	BET 1834 AND 1835, Buncombe County, North Carolina[2]

Father:	**Uriah WARREN Sr.** (BET 1809 AND 1810-aft 1880)
Mother:	**Susan Tabitha MORGAN** (abt 1804-BET 1839 AND 1840)

Spouse:	**Joseph WARREN** (BET 1800 AND 1840-)
Birth:	BET 1800 AND 1840[2]
Marriage:	8 Oct 1858, Buncombe County, North Carolina[3]

1.1.1.3 Josiah WARREN[1,2]

Birth:	BET 1834 AND 1835, Buncombe County, North Carolina[2]
Father:	**Uriah WARREN Sr.** (BET 1809 AND 1810-aft 1880)
Mother:	**Susan Tabitha MORGAN** (abt 1804-BET 1839 AND 1840)

1.1.1.4 Uriah WARREN Jr.[1,2]

Birth:	BET 1836 AND 1837, Buncombe County, North Carolina[2]
Father:	**Uriah WARREN Sr.** (BET 1809 AND 1810-aft 1880)
Mother:	**Susan Tabitha MORGAN** (abt 1804-BET 1839 AND 1840)

Spouse:	**Elizabeth GOODSON** (BET 1835 AND 1846-)
Birth:	BET 1835 AND 1846[2]
Marriage:	4 Mar 1861, Buncombe County, North Carolina[3]

1.1.1.5 William H. WARREN[1,2]

Birth:	BET 1838 AND 1839, Buncombe County, North Carolina[2]
Father:	**Uriah WARREN Sr.** (BET 1809 AND 1810-aft 1880)
Mother:	**Susan Tabitha MORGAN** (abt 1804-BET 1839 AND 1840)

Spouse:	**N. M. WRIGHT** (BET 1835 AND 1845-)
Birth:	BET 1835 AND 1845[2]
Marriage:	23 Mar 1860, Buncombe County, North Carolina[3]

1.1.2 Permenter D. MORGAN Sr.[1,2]

Birth:	26 Jun 1806, Rutherford County, North Carolina[2]
Death:	29 Jan 1865, Petersburg, Virginia (during the Civil War)[2]
Father:	**James Squire MORGAN** (27 Oct 1780-25 Oct 1854)
Mother:	**Margaret (Peggy) GRANT** (abt 1788-10 Sep 1845)

Spouse:	**Charity YOUNG** (8 Jan 1808-13 Sep 1870)
Birth:	8 Jan 1808[2]
Death:	13 Sep 1870[2]

Marriage: BET 1820 AND 1829, Buncombe County, North Carolina[3]

8 Children...
      Elisha Wilson (16 Jan 1829-3 Feb 1864)
      James M. (BET 1830 AND 1831-)
      William (31 Jul 1836-1 Mar 1905)
      Permenter D. Jr. (2 May 1842-12 Oct 1922)
      Margaret (BET 1844 AND 1845-)
      Charity (10 May 1847-12 Dec 1917)
      Stacy (BET 1849 AND 1850-)
      Lavada (abt Feb 1856-)

1.1.2.1 Elisha Wilson MORGAN[1,2]

Birth: 16 Jan 1829, Buncombe County, North Carolina[2]
Death: 3 Feb 1864, Virginia (during the Civil War)[2]
Father: **Permenter D. MORGAN Sr.** (26 Jun 1806-29 Jan 1865)
Mother: **Charity YOUNG** (8 Jan 1808-13 Sep 1870)

Spouse: **Nancy SMATHERS** (30 Jun 1835-29 Aug 1871)
Birth: 30 Jun 1835[2]
Death: 29 Aug 1871[2]
Marriage: 16 Feb 1854, Buncombe County, North Carolina[3]

1.1.2.2 James M. MORGAN[1,2]

Birth: BET 1830 AND 1831, Buncombe County, North Carolina[2]
Father: **Permenter D. MORGAN Sr.** (26 Jun 1806-29 Jan 1865)
Mother: **Charity YOUNG** (8 Jan 1808-13 Sep 1870)

Spouse: **Nancy JOYCE**

1.1.2.3 William MORGAN[1,2]

Birth: 31 Jul 1836, Buncombe County, North Carolina[2]
Death: 1 Mar 1905[2]
Father: **Permenter D. MORGAN Sr.** (26 Jun 1806-29 Jan 1865)
Mother: **Charity YOUNG** (8 Jan 1808-13 Sep 1870)

Spouse: **Rebecca YOUNG** (27 Oct 1839-20 Oct 1916)
Birth: 27 Oct 1839[2]
Death: 20 Oct 1916[2]

1.1.2.4 Permenter D. MORGAN Jr.[1,2]

Birth:	2 May 1842, Buncombe County, North Carolina[2]
Death:	12 Oct 1922[2]
Father:	**Permenter D. MORGAN Sr.** (26 Jun 1806-29 Jan 1865)
Mother:	**Charity YOUNG** (8 Jan 1808-13 Sep 1870)

1.1.2.5 Margaret MORGAN[1,2]

Birth:	BET 1844 AND 1845, Buncombe County, North Carolina[2]
Father:	**Permenter D. MORGAN Sr.** (26 Jun 1806-29 Jan 1865)
Mother:	**Charity YOUNG** (8 Jan 1808-13 Sep 1870)
Spouse:	**John LUTHER** (BET 1800 AND 1850-)
Birth:	BET 1800 AND 1850[2]

1.1.2.6 Charity MORGAN[1,2]

Birth:	10 May 1847, Buncombe County, North Carolina[2]
Death:	12 Dec 1917[2]
Father:	**Permenter D. MORGAN Sr.** (26 Jun 1806-29 Jan 1865)
Mother:	**Charity YOUNG** (8 Jan 1808-13 Sep 1870)
Spouse:	**William Edward JONES** (abt 1844-abt 1941)
Birth:	abt 1844[2]
Death:	abt 1941[2]

1.1.2.7 Stacy MORGAN[1,2]

Birth:	BET 1849 AND 1850, Buncombe County, North Carolina[2]
Father:	**Permenter D. MORGAN Sr.** (26 Jun 1806-29 Jan 1865)
Mother:	**Charity YOUNG** (8 Jan 1808-13 Sep 1870)

1.1.2.8 Lavada MORGAN[1,2]

Birth:	abt Feb 1856, Buncombe County, North Carolina[2]
Father:	**Permenter D. MORGAN Sr.** (26 Jun 1806-29 Jan 1865)
Mother:	**Charity YOUNG** (8 Jan 1808-13 Sep 1870)
Spouse:	**J. Lee THRASH** (BET 1830 AND 1860-)
Birth:	BET 1830 AND 1860[2]
Marriage:	31 Aug 1869, Buncombe County, North Carolina[3]

1.1.3 Mary (Polly) MORGAN[1,2]

Birth:	abt 1808, Rutherford County, North Carolina[2]
Death:	27 Jan 1877, Buncombe County, North Carolina[2]
Father:	**James Squire MORGAN** (27 Oct 1780-25 Oct 1854)
Mother:	**Margaret (Peggy) GRANT** (abt 1788-10 Sep 1845)

1.1.4a Morris Grant MORGAN Sr.*[1,2]

Birth:	BET 1809 AND 1810, Buncombe County, North Carolina[2]
Father:	**James Squire MORGAN** (27 Oct 1780-25 Oct 1854)
Mother:	**Margaret (Peggy) GRANT** (abt 1788-10 Sep 1845)
Spouse:	**Margaret (Peggy) MORGAN** (BET 1819 AND 1820-)
Birth:	BET 1819 AND 1820, Rutherford County, North Carolina[2]
Father:	**Jesse MORGAN** (28 Oct 1785-30 Oct 1858)
Mother:	**Mary (Polly) GRANT** (abt 1793-abt 1831)
Marriage:	BET 1830 AND 1837, Buncombe County, North Carolina[1,3]

9 Children...
> **Rebecca** (BET 1834 AND 1835-)
> **Jonathan** (BET 1835 AND 1836-)
> **Martha** (abt 1837-abt 1924)
> **Margaret** (BET 1837 AND 1838-)
> **James** (BET 1841 AND 1842-)
> **Enoch** (BET 1843 AND 1844-)
> **Mary** (BET 1846 AND 1847-)
> **Lucinda** (BET 1851 AND 1859-)
> **Morris Grant Jr.** (22 May 1851-)

Other spouses: Elizabeth TAYLOR

1.1.4a.1 Rebecca MORGAN[4,2]

Birth:	BET 1834 AND 1835, Buncombe County, North Carolina[2]
Father:	**Morris Grant MORGAN Sr.** (BET 1809 AND 1810-)
Mother:	**Margaret (Peggy) MORGAN** (BET 1819 AND 1820-)
Spouse:	**Robert H. PARKER** (BET 1800 AND 1840-)
Birth:	BET 1800 AND 1840[2]
Marriage:	14 Feb 1856, Union County, Georgia[3]

1.1.4a.2 Jonathan MORGAN[4,2]

Birth:	BET 1835 AND 1836, Buncombe County, North Carolina[2]
Father:	**Morris Grant MORGAN Sr.** (BET 1809 AND 1810-)
Mother:	**Margaret (Peggy) MORGAN** (BET 1819 AND 1820-)

1.1.4a.3 Martha MORGAN[4,2]

Birth:	abt 1837[2]
Death:	abt 1924[2]
Father:	**Morris Grant MORGAN Sr.** (BET 1809 AND 1810-)
Mother:	**Margaret (Peggy) MORGAN** (BET 1819 AND 1820-)
Spouse:	**William PEEBLES** (abt 1838-abt 1910)
Birth:	abt 1838[2]
Death:	abt 1910[2]
Marriage:	bef 1850, Union County, Georgia[1,3]

1.1.4a.4 Margaret MORGAN[4,2]

Birth:	BET 1837 AND 1838, Buncombe County, North Carolina[2]
Father:	**Morris Grant MORGAN Sr.** (BET 1809 AND 1810-)
Mother:	**Margaret (Peggy) MORGAN** (BET 1819 AND 1820-)

1.1.4a.5 James MORGAN[4,2]

Birth:	BET 1841 AND 1842, Buncombe County, North Carolina[2]
Father:	**Morris Grant MORGAN Sr.** (BET 1809 AND 1810-)
Mother:	**Margaret (Peggy) MORGAN** (BET 1819 AND 1820-)

1.1.4a.6 Enoch MORGAN[4,2]

Birth:	BET 1843 AND 1844, Union County, Georgia[2]
Father:	**Morris Grant MORGAN Sr.** (BET 1809 AND 1810-)
Mother:	**Margaret (Peggy) MORGAN** (BET 1819 AND 1820-)

1.1.4a.7 Mary MORGAN[4,2]

Birth:	BET 1846 AND 1847, Union County, Georgia[2]
Father:	**Morris Grant MORGAN Sr.** (BET 1809 AND 1810-)
Mother:	**Margaret (Peggy) MORGAN** (BET 1819 AND 1820-)

1.1.4a.8 Lucinda MORGAN[4,2]

Birth: BET 1851 AND 1859[2]
Father: **Morris Grant MORGAN Sr.** (BET 1809 AND 1810-)
Mother: **Margaret (Peggy) MORGAN** (BET 1819 AND 1820-)

1.1.4a.9 Morris Grant MORGAN Jr.[4,2]

Birth: 22 May 1851, Union County, Georgia[2]
Father: **Morris Grant MORGAN Sr.** (BET 1809 AND 1810-)
Mother: **Margaret (Peggy) MORGAN** (BET 1819 AND 1820-)

Spouse: **Rachel OWENBY** (BET 1850 AND 1875-)
Birth: BET 1850 AND 1875[2]
Marriage: aft 1866[3]

1.1.4b Morris Grant MORGAN Sr.* (See above)

Spouse: **Elizabeth TAYLOR** (BET 1800 AND 1830-)
Birth: BET 1800 AND 1830[2]
Marriage: aft 1859[3]

4 Children...
         William Permenter (abt 1860-abt 1926)
         Elijah (aft 1860-)
         Jefferson L. (abt 1862-abt 1926)
         Elizabeth (abt 1864-)

Other spouses: Margaret (Peggy) MORGAN

1.1.4b.1 William Permenter MORGAN[1,2]

Birth: abt 1860[2]
Death: abt 1926[2]
Father: **Morris Grant MORGAN Sr.** (BET 1809 AND 1810-)
Mother: **Elizabeth TAYLOR** (BET 1800 AND 1830-)

Spouse: **Emiline McCLURE** (BET 1855 AND 1880-)
Birth: BET 1855 AND 1880[2]
Marriage: aft 1875[3]

1.1.4b.2 Elijah MORGAN[1,2]

Birth: aft 1860[2]

Father:	**Morris Grant MORGAN Sr.** (BET 1809 AND 1810-)
Mother:	**Elizabeth TAYLOR** (BET 1800 AND 1830-)

1.1.4b.3a Jefferson L. MORGAN*[1,2]

Birth:	abt 1862[2]
Death:	abt 1926[2]
Father:	**Morris Grant MORGAN Sr.** (BET 1809 AND 1810-)
Mother:	**Elizabeth TAYLOR** (BET 1800 AND 1830-)
Spouse:	**Angline BYERS** (BET 1860 AND 1880-)
Birth:	BET 1860 AND 1880[2]
Marriage:	aft 1888[3]

Other spouses: Jennie Majors GILSTRAP

1.1.4b.3b Jefferson L. MORGAN* (See above)

Spouse:	**Jennie Majors GILSTRAP** (BET 1860 AND 1890-)
Birth:	BET 1860 AND 1890[2]
Marriage:	aft 1889[3]

Other spouses: Angline BYERS

1.1.4b.4 Elizabeth MORGAN[1,2]

Birth:	abt 1864[2]
Father:	**Morris Grant MORGAN Sr.** (BET 1809 AND 1810-)
Mother:	**Elizabeth TAYLOR** (BET 1800 AND 1830-)
Spouse:	**Daniel NICHOLS** (BET 1840 AND 1870-)
Birth:	BET 1840 AND 1870[2]
Marriage:	aft 1880[3]

1.1.5 Jones H. MORGAN[1,2]

Birth:	4 Sep 1812, Buncombe County, North Carolina[2]
Death:	16 Jul 1854, Buncombe County, North Carolina[2]
Father:	**James Squire MORGAN** (27 Oct 1780-25 Oct 1854)
Mother:	**Margaret (Peggy) GRANT** (abt 1788-10 Sep 1845)
Spouse:	**Rebecca YOUNG** (18 Jun 1818-17 Jun 1888)

Birth:	18 Jun 1818, Buncombe County, North Carolina[2]
Death:	17 Jun 1888, Buncombe County, North Carolina[2]
Birth:	18 Jun 1818[2]
Marriage:	5 Jan 1836, Rutherford County, North Carolina[1,3]

7 Children...
> **Carolina** (BET 1836 AND 1837-)
> **Rebecca A.** (BET 1839 AND 1840-BET 1861 AND 1867)
> **Jonathan L.** (BET 1842 AND 1843-)
> **Wilson** (BET 1844 AND 1845-)
> **Jones H.** (BET 1846 AND 1849-)
> **Martha E.** (BET 1848 AND 1849-)
> **Marion** (BET 1854 AND 1855-)

1.1.5.1 Carolina MORGAN[1,2]

Birth:	BET 1836 AND 1837[2]
Father:	**Jones H. MORGAN** (4 Sep 1812-16 Jul 1854)
Mother:	**Rebecca YOUNG** (18 Jun 1818-17 Jun 1888)

Spouse:	**Jeremiah GREEN Jr.** (11 Nov 1830-)
Birth:	11 Nov 1830, Buncombe County, North Carolina[2]
Father:	**Jeremiah GREEN Sr.** (BET 1780 AND 1800-)
Mother:	**Katherine HAGAMAN** (BET 1780 AND 1800-)
Marriage:	26 Nov 1857, Buncombe County, North Carolina[3]

1.1.5.2 Rebecca A. MORGAN[1,2]

Birth:	BET 1839 AND 1840, Buncombe County, North Carolina[2]
Death:	BET 1861 AND 1867, Buncombe County, North Carolina[2]
Father:	**Jones H. MORGAN** (4 Sep 1812-16 Jul 1854)
Mother:	**Rebecca YOUNG** (18 Jun 1818-17 Jun 1888)

Spouse:	**Silas M. MORGAN** (10 Jun 1818-11 Oct 1896)
Birth:	10 Jun 1818, Rutherford County, North Carolina[2]
Death:	11 Oct 1896, Buncombe County, North Carolina[2]
Father:	**Jesse MORGAN** (28 Oct 1785-30 Oct 1858)
Mother:	**Mary (Polly) GRANT** (abt 1793-abt 1831)
Marriage:	13 Dec 1859, Buncombe County, North Carolina[1,3]

2 Children...
> **Silas Lafayette** (BET 1858 AND 1859-)
> **Rebecca** (BET 1860 AND 1861-)

1.1.5.2.1 Silas Lafayette MORGAN[5,2]

Birth:	BET 1858 AND 1859, Buncombe County, North Carolina[2]
Father:	**Silas M. MORGAN** (10 Jun 1818-11 Oct 1896)
Mother:	**Rebecca A. MORGAN** (BET 1839 AND 1840-BET 1861 AND 1867)

Spouse:	**Elmira MORGAN** (BET 1870 AND 1871-)
Birth:	BET 1870 AND 1871, Buncombe County, North Carolina[2]
Marriage:	24 Dec 1895, Buncombe County, North Carolina[5,3]

1.1.5.2.2 Rebecca MORGAN[5,2]

Birth:	BET 1860 AND 1861, Buncombe County, North Carolina[2]
Father:	**Silas M. MORGAN** (10 Jun 1818-11 Oct 1896)
Mother:	**Rebecca A. MORGAN** (BET 1839 AND 1840-BET 1861 AND 1867)

Spouse:	**G. W. CHANDLER** (BET 1879 AND 1880-)
Birth:	BET 1879 AND 1880, Buncombe County, North Carolina[2]
Marriage:	25 Oct 1884, Buncombe County, North Carolina[5,3]

1.1.5.3 Jonathan L. MORGAN[1,2]

Birth:	BET 1842 AND 1843, Buncombe County, North Carolina[2]
Father:	**Jones H. MORGAN** (4 Sep 1812-16 Jul 1854)
Mother:	**Rebecca YOUNG** (18 Jun 1818-17 Jun 1888)

Spouse:	**Jane WIFE OF JONATHON L. MORGAN** (BET 1840 AND 1880-)
Birth:	BET 1840 AND 1880[2]
Marriage:	aft 1860[3]

1.1.5.4 Wilson MORGAN[1,2]

Birth:	BET 1844 AND 1845, Buncombe County, North Carolina[2]
Father:	**Jones H. MORGAN** (4 Sep 1812-16 Jul 1854)
Mother:	**Rebecca YOUNG** (18 Jun 1818-17 Jun 1888)

1.1.5.5 Jones H. MORGAN[1,2]

Birth:	BET 1846 AND 1849, Buncombe County, North Carolina[2]

Father: **Jones H. MORGAN** (4 Sep 1812-16 Jul 1854)
Mother: **Rebecca YOUNG** (18 Jun 1818-17 Jun 1888)

Spouse: **Mary L. WIFE OF JONES H. MORGAN** (BET 1840 AND 1870-)
Birth: BET 1840 AND 1870[2]
Marriage: aft 1860[3]

1.1.5.6 Martha E. MORGAN[1,2]

Birth: BET 1848 AND 1849, Buncombe County, North Carolina[2]
Father: **Jones H. MORGAN** (4 Sep 1812-16 Jul 1854)
Mother: **Rebecca YOUNG** (18 Jun 1818-17 Jun 1888)

1.1.5.7 Marion MORGAN[1,2]

Birth: BET 1854 AND 1855, Buncombe County, North Carolina[2]
Father: **Jones H. MORGAN** (4 Sep 1812-16 Jul 1854)
Mother: **Rebecca YOUNG** (18 Jun 1818-17 Jun 1888)

1.1.6 Margaret MORGAN[1,2]

Birth: BET 1813 AND 1814, Buncombe County, North Carolina[2]
Death: abt 1870[2]
Father: **James Squire MORGAN** (27 Oct 1780-25 Oct 1854)
Mother: **Margaret (Peggy) GRANT** (abt 1788-10 Sep 1845)

Spouse: **William HUMPHRIES** (BET 1810 AND 1811-abt 1871)
Birth: BET 1810 AND 1811, South Carolina[2]
Death: abt 1871[2]
Marriage: BET 1830 AND 1832, Buncombe County, North Carolina[3]

8 Children...
    Sarah (BET 1833 AND 1834-)
    Permenter (BET 1834 AND 1841-)
    Margaret (BET 1835 AND 1836-)
    James (BET 1837 AND 1838-)
    Pinkney (BET 1842 AND 1843-)
    Elizabeth (BET 1844 AND 1845-)
    Mary (BET 1846 AND 1847-)
    Caroline (BET 1848 AND 1849-)

1.1.6.1 Sarah HUMPHRIES[5,2]

Birth: BET 1833 AND 1834, Buncombe County, North Carolina[2]
Father: **William HUMPHRIES** (BET 1810 AND 1811-abt 1871)
Mother: **Margaret MORGAN** (BET 1813 AND 1814-abt 1870)

1.1.6.2 Permenter HUMPHRIES[5,2]

Birth: BET 1834 AND 1841, Buncombe County, North Carolina[2]
Father: **William HUMPHRIES** (BET 1810 AND 1811-abt 1871)
Mother: **Margaret MORGAN** (BET 1813 AND 1814-abt 1870)

1.1.6.3 Margaret HUMPHRIES[5,2]

Birth: BET 1835 AND 1836, Buncombe County, North Carolina[2]
Father: **William HUMPHRIES** (BET 1810 AND 1811-abt 1871)
Mother: **Margaret MORGAN** (BET 1813 AND 1814-abt 1870)

1.1.6.4 James HUMPHRIES[5,2]

Birth: BET 1837 AND 1838, Buncombe County, North Carolina[2]
Father: **William HUMPHRIES** (BET 1810 AND 1811-abt 1871)
Mother: **Margaret MORGAN** (BET 1813 AND 1814-abt 1870)

1.1.6.5 Pinkney HUMPHRIES[5,2]

Birth: BET 1842 AND 1843, Buncombe County, North Carolina[2]
Father: **William HUMPHRIES** (BET 1810 AND 1811-abt 1871)
Mother: **Margaret MORGAN** (BET 1813 AND 1814-abt 1870)

1.1.6.6 Elizabeth HUMPHRIES[5,2]

Birth: BET 1844 AND 1845, Buncombe County, North Carolina[2]
Father: **William HUMPHRIES** (BET 1810 AND 1811-abt 1871)
Mother: **Margaret MORGAN** (BET 1813 AND 1814-abt 1870)

1.1.6.7 Mary HUMPHRIES[5,2]

Birth: BET 1846 AND 1847, Buncombe County, North Carolina[2]
Father: **William HUMPHRIES** (BET 1810 AND 1811-abt 1871)
Mother: **Margaret MORGAN** (BET 1813 AND 1814-abt 1870)

1.1.6.8 Caroline HUMPHRIES[1,2]

Birth: BET 1848 AND 1849, Buncombe County, North Carolina[2]

Father:	**William HUMPHRIES** (BET 1810 AND 1811-abt 1871)
Mother:	**Margaret MORGAN** (BET 1813 AND 1814-abt 1870)

1.1.7 Lewis R. MORGAN[1,2]

Birth:	BET 1816 AND 1817, Buncombe County, North Carolina[2]
Death:	aft 1880, Buncombe County, North Carolina[2]
Father:	**James Squire MORGAN** (27 Oct 1780-25 Oct 1854)
Mother:	**Margaret (Peggy) GRANT** (abt 1788-10 Sep 1845)
Spouse:	**Grace MORGAN** (2 Feb 1821-11 Jan 1919)
Birth:	2 Feb 1821, Buncombe County, North Carolina[2]
Death:	11 Jan 1919[2]
Father:	**Jonathon MORGAN** (BET 1780 AND 1805-)
Mother:	**Rebecca WILKERSON** (BET 1780 AND 1805-)
Marriage:	2 Oct 1839, Rutherford County, North Carolina[5,3]

13 Children...
> **Rebecca** (BET 1839 AND 1840-)
> **James** (BET 1841 AND 1842-)
> **Margaret L.** (BET 1842 AND 1843-)
> **Pinkney** (BET 1843 AND 1844-)
> **Lewis Webster** (BET 1847 AND 1848-)
> **Permenter S.** (BET 1850 AND 1851-)
> **Moses S.** (BET 1852 AND 1853-)
> **Mary C.** (BET 1854 AND 1855-)
> **Enoch J.** (BET 1856 AND 1857-)
> **Noah** (BET 1857 AND 1858-)
> **Elizabeth** (abt 1860-)
> **Martha** (BET 1862 AND 1863-)
> **Thomas** (BET 1866 AND 1867-)

1.1.7.1 Rebecca MORGAN[5,2]

Birth:	BET 1839 AND 1840, Buncombe County, North Carolina[2]
Father:	**Lewis R. MORGAN** (BET 1816 AND 1817-aft 1880)
Mother:	**Grace MORGAN** (2 Feb 1821-11 Jan 1919)

1.1.7.2 James MORGAN[5,2]

Birth:	BET 1841 AND 1842, Buncombe County, North Carolina[2]
Father:	**Lewis R. MORGAN** (BET 1816 AND 1817-aft 1880)
Mother:	**Grace MORGAN** (2 Feb 1821-11 Jan 1919)

1.1.7.3 Margaret L. MORGAN[5,2]

Birth:	BET 1842 AND 1843, Buncombe County, North Carolina[2]
Father:	**Lewis R. MORGAN** (BET 1816 AND 1817-aft 1880)
Mother:	**Grace MORGAN** (2 Feb 1821-11 Jan 1919)

Spouse:	**Jeptha Irenious MILLER** (6 Jul 1840-14 Oct 1901)
Birth:	6 Jul 1840, Buncombe County, North Carolina[2]
Death:	14 Oct 1901, Buncombe County, North Carolina[2]

1.1.7.4 Pinkney MORGAN[5,2]

Birth:	BET 1843 AND 1844, Buncombe County, North Carolina[2]
Father:	**Lewis R. MORGAN** (BET 1816 AND 1817-aft 1880)
Mother:	**Grace MORGAN** (2 Feb 1821-11 Jan 1919)

1.1.7.5 Lewis Webster MORGAN[5,2]

Birth:	BET 1847 AND 1848, Buncombe County, North Carolina[2]
Father:	**Lewis R. MORGAN** (BET 1816 AND 1817-aft 1880)
Mother:	**Grace MORGAN** (2 Feb 1821-11 Jan 1919)

Spouse:	**Margaret M. MILLER** (BET 1845 AND 1860-)
Birth:	BET 1845 AND 1860[2]
Marriage:	aft 1867[3]

1.1.7.6 Permenter S. MORGAN[5,2]

Birth:	BET 1850 AND 1851, Buncombe County, North Carolina[2]
Father:	**Lewis R. MORGAN** (BET 1816 AND 1817-aft 1880)
Mother:	**Grace MORGAN** (2 Feb 1821-11 Jan 1919)

Spouse:	**Mary (Polly) A. MILLER** (BET 1847 AND 1848-)
Birth:	BET 1847 AND 1848, Buncombe County, North Carolina[2]
Father:	**Henry H. MILLER** (BET 1800 AND 1835-)
Mother:	**Rachel WARREN** (BET 1800 AND 1835-)
Marriage:	11 Mar 1877, Buncombe County, North Carolina[5,3]

1.1.7.7 Moses S. MORGAN[5,2]

Birth:	BET 1852 AND 1853, Buncombe County, North Carolina[2]
Father:	**Lewis R. MORGAN** (BET 1816 AND 1817-aft 1880)

Mother:	**Grace MORGAN** (2 Feb 1821-11 Jan 1919)
Spouse:	**Mary E. THOMPSON** (BET 1867 AND 1868-)
Birth:	BET 1867 AND 1868[2]
Marriage:	29 Feb 1888, Buncombe County, North Carolina[5,3]

1.1.7.8 Mary C. MORGAN[5,2]

Birth:	BET 1854 AND 1855, Buncombe County, North Carolina[2]
Father:	**Lewis R. MORGAN** (BET 1816 AND 1817-aft 1880)
Mother:	**Grace MORGAN** (2 Feb 1821-11 Jan 1919)
Spouse:	**W. M. JONES** (BET 1856 AND 1857-)
Birth:	BET 1856 AND 1857, Buncombe County, North Carolina[2]
Marriage:	20 Nov 1880, Buncombe County, North Carolina[5,3]

1.1.7.9 Enoch J. MORGAN[5,2]

Birth:	BET 1856 AND 1857[2]
Father:	**Lewis R. MORGAN** (BET 1816 AND 1817-aft 1880)
Mother:	**Grace MORGAN** (2 Feb 1821-11 Jan 1919)
Spouse:	**Mary (Polly) Ann MORGAN** (BET 1856 AND 1857-)
Birth:	BET 1856 AND 1857, Buncombe County, North Carolina[2]
Father:	**Silas M. MORGAN** (10 Jun 1818-11 Oct 1896)
Mother:	**Sarah Myra GRANT** (BET 1832 AND 1833-abt 1858)
Marriage:	16 Jan 1879, Buncombe County, North Carolina[5,3]

1.1.7.10 Noah MORGAN[5,2]

Birth:	BET 1857 AND 1858, Buncombe County, North Carolina[2]
Father:	**Lewis R. MORGAN** (BET 1816 AND 1817-aft 1880)
Mother:	**Grace MORGAN** (2 Feb 1821-11 Jan 1919)
Spouse:	**Vicie (Vickie?) JONES** (BET 1860 AND 1861-)
Birth:	BET 1860 AND 1861, Buncombe County, North Carolina[2]
Marriage:	10 Mar 1882, Buncombe County, North Carolina[5,3]

1.1.7.11 Elizabeth MORGAN[5,2]

Birth:	abt 1860, Buncombe County, North Carolina[2]
Father:	**Lewis R. MORGAN** (BET 1816 AND 1817-aft 1880)
Mother:	**Grace MORGAN** (2 Feb 1821-11 Jan 1919)

1.1.7.12 Martha MORGAN[5,2]

Birth: BET 1862 AND 1863, Buncombe County, North Carolina[2]
Father: **Lewis R. MORGAN** (BET 1816 AND 1817-aft 1880)
Mother: **Grace MORGAN** (2 Feb 1821-11 Jan 1919)

1.1.7.13 Thomas MORGAN[5,2]

Birth: BET 1866 AND 1867, Buncombe County, North Carolina[2]
Father: **Lewis R. MORGAN** (BET 1816 AND 1817-aft 1880)
Mother: **Grace MORGAN** (2 Feb 1821-11 Jan 1919)

Spouse: **Minnie HALL** (BET 1866 AND 1867-)
Birth: BET 1866 AND 1867, Buncombe County, North Carolina[2]
Marriage: 5 Jun 1887, Buncombe County, North Carolina[5,3]

1.1.8 Martha MORGAN[1,2]

Birth: abt 1817, Buncombe County, North Carolina[2]
Father: **James Squire MORGAN** (27 Oct 1780-25 Oct 1854)
Mother: **Margaret (Peggy) GRANT** (abt 1788-10 Sep 1845)

Spouse: **Robert WARREN** (BET 1824 AND 1825-)
Birth: BET 1824 AND 1825, Buncombe County, North Carolina[2]
Marriage: BET 1840 AND 1843, Buncombe County, North Carolina[5,3]

6 Children...
     Naomi (BET 1845 AND 1846-)
     Margaret (BET 1845 AND 1846-22 Jun 1937)
     James (BET 1848 AND 1849-)
     William Lafayette (9 Jul 1852-)
     R. Morris (BET 1854 AND 1855-)
     Elberry (26 Dec 1861-25 Jun 1936)

1.1.8.1 Naomi WARREN[5,2]

Birth: BET 1845 AND 1846, Buncombe County, North Carolina[2]
Father: **Robert WARREN** (BET 1824 AND 1825-)
Mother: **Martha MORGAN** (abt 1817-)

1.1.8.2 Margaret WARREN[5,2]

Birth:	BET 1845 AND 1846, Buncombe County, North Carolina[2]
Death:	22 Jun 1937[2]
Father:	**Robert WARREN** (BET 1824 AND 1825-)
Mother:	**Martha MORGAN** (abt 1817-)

Spouse:	**Andrew Jackson DAVIS** (17 Apr 1832-24 May 1929)
Birth:	17 Apr 1832[2]
Death:	24 May 1929[2]
Marriage:	21 Dec 1859, Buncombe County, North Carolina[5,3]

1.1.8.3 James WARREN[5,2]

Birth:	BET 1848 AND 1849, Buncombe County, North Carolina[2]
Father:	**Robert WARREN** (BET 1824 AND 1825-)
Mother:	**Martha MORGAN** (abt 1817-)

Spouse:	**Hannah DAVIS** (BET 1850 AND 1880-)
Birth:	BET 1850 AND 1880[2]
Marriage:	aft 1862[3]

1.1.8.4 William Lafayette WARREN[5,2]

Birth:	9 Jul 1852, Buncombe County, North Carolina[2]
Father:	**Robert WARREN** (BET 1824 AND 1825-)
Mother:	**Martha MORGAN** (abt 1817-)

Spouse:	**Martha Elmira DAVIS** (BET 1850 AND 1880-)
Birth:	BET 1850 AND 1880[2]
Marriage:	aft 1868[3]

1.1.8.5 R. Morris WARREN[5,2]

Birth:	BET 1854 AND 1855, Buncombe County, North Carolina[2]
Father:	**Robert WARREN** (BET 1824 AND 1825-)
Mother:	**Martha MORGAN** (abt 1817-)

Spouse:	**Julia NEAL** (BET 1850 AND 1880-)
Birth:	BET 1850 AND 1880[2]
Marriage:	aft 1870[3]

1.1.8.6 Elberry WARREN[5,2]

Birth:	26 Dec 1861, Buncombe County, North Carolina[2]

Death:	25 Jun 1936[2]
Father:	**Robert WARREN** (BET 1824 AND 1825-)
Mother:	**Martha MORGAN** (abt 1817-)

Spouse:	**Mary Ann PEEBLES** (5 Sep 1861-)
Birth:	5 Sep 1861[2]
Marriage:	26 Oct 1883, Buncombe County, North Carolina[5,3]

1.1.9 James MORGAN[1,2]

Birth:	1 Feb 1820, Buncombe County, North Carolina[2]
Death:	1 Apr 1891, Buncombe County, North Carolina[2]
Father:	**James Squire MORGAN** (27 Oct 1780-25 Oct 1854)
Mother:	**Margaret (Peggy) GRANT** (abt 1788-10 Sep 1845)

Spouse:	**Hannah Amanda WARREN** (25 Feb 1829-6 Sep 1902)
Birth:	25 Feb 1829, Buncombe County, North Carolina[2]
Death:	6 Sep 1902, Buncombe County, North Carolina[2]
Marriage:	BET 1840 AND 1850, Buncombe County, North Carolina[3]

4 Children...
Mary J. (BET 1851 AND 1852-)
George W. (BET 1853 AND 1854-)
Margaret (BET 1856 AND 1857-)
Martha (BET 1858 AND 1859-)

1.1.9.1 Mary J. MORGAN[5,2]

Birth:	BET 1851 AND 1852, Buncombe County, North Carolina[2]
Father:	**James MORGAN** (1 Feb 1820-1 Apr 1891)
Mother:	**Hannah Amanda WARREN** (25 Feb 1829-6 Sep 1902)

1.1.9.2 George W. MORGAN[5,2]

Birth:	BET 1853 AND 1854, Buncombe County, North Carolina[2]
Father:	**James MORGAN** (1 Feb 1820-1 Apr 1891)
Mother:	**Hannah Amanda WARREN** (25 Feb 1829-6 Sep 1902)

Spouse:	**Caroline SAWYER** (BET 1869 AND 1870-)
Birth:	BET 1869 AND 1870, Buncombe County, North Carolina[2]
Marriage:	28 Oct 1888, Buncombe County, North Carolina[5,3]

1.1.9.3 Margaret MORGAN[5,2]

Birth:	BET 1856 AND 1857, Buncombe County, North Carolina[2]
Father:	**James MORGAN** (1 Feb 1820-1 Apr 1891)
Mother:	**Hannah Amanda WARREN** (25 Feb 1829-6 Sep 1902)

1.1.9.4 Martha MORGAN[5,2]

Birth:	BET 1858 AND 1859, Buncombe County, North Carolina[2]
Father:	**James MORGAN** (1 Feb 1820-1 Apr 1891)
Mother:	**Hannah Amanda WARREN** (25 Feb 1829-6 Sep 1902)

1.1.10 Millie MORGAN[1,2]

Birth:	abt 1822, Buncombe County, North Carolina[2]
Father:	**James Squire MORGAN** (27 Oct 1780-25 Oct 1854)
Mother:	**Margaret (Peggy) GRANT** (abt 1788-10 Sep 1845)
Spouse:	**Reverend James THOMPSON** (BET 1800 AND 1830-)
Birth:	BET 1800 AND 1830
Marriage:	BET 1840 AND 1850, Buncombe County, North Carolina[3]

1.1.11 Elijah MORGAN[1,2]

Birth:	9 Aug 1824, Buncombe County, North Carolina[2]
Death:	27 Oct 1879, Buncombe County, North Carolina[2]
Father:	**James Squire MORGAN** (27 Oct 1780-25 Oct 1854)
Mother:	**Margaret (Peggy) GRANT** (abt 1788-10 Sep 1845)
Spouse:	**Jane GREEN** (11 Sep 1828-18 Jan 1890)
Birth:	11 Sep 1828, Buncombe County, North Carolina[2]
Death:	18 Jan 1890, Buncombe County, North Carolina[2]
Father:	**Jeremiah GREEN Sr.** (BET 1780 AND 1800-)
Mother:	**Katherine HAGAMAN** (BET 1780 AND 1800-)
Marriage:	3 Feb 1848, Buncombe County, North Carolina[3]

10 Children...
> **James Wilson** (BET 1848 AND 1849-)
> **Jeremiah** (BET 1850 AND 1851-)
> **Tilitha** (BET 1853 AND 1854-)
> **Columbus M.** (BET 1855 AND 1856-)
> **Richard Cansler** (BET 1857 AND 1858-)
> **Laura J.** (abt 1859-)
> **George L.** (BET 1860 AND 1861-)

Bilton (BET 1862 AND 1863-)
Texas E. (BET 1866 AND 1867-)
Etta (BET 1874 AND 1875-)

1.1.11.1 James Wilson MORGAN[5,2]

Birth:	BET 1848 AND 1849, Buncombe County, North Carolina[2]
Father:	**Elijah MORGAN** (9 Aug 1824-27 Oct 1879)
Mother:	**Jane GREEN** (11 Sep 1828-18 Jan 1890)

1.1.11.2 Jeremiah MORGAN[5,2]

Birth:	BET 1850 AND 1851, Buncombe County, North Carolina[2]
Father:	**Elijah MORGAN** (9 Aug 1824-27 Oct 1879)
Mother:	**Jane GREEN** (11 Sep 1828-18 Jan 1890)
Spouse:	**Dicie Ann CATHEY** (BET 1850 AND 1880-)
Birth:	BET 1850 AND 1880[2]
Marriage:	aft 1865[3]

1.1.11.3 Tilitha MORGAN[5,2]

Birth:	BET 1853 AND 1854, Buncombe County, North Carolina[2]
Father:	**Elijah MORGAN** (9 Aug 1824-27 Oct 1879)
Mother:	**Jane GREEN** (11 Sep 1828-18 Jan 1890)

1.1.11.4 Columbus M. MORGAN[5,2]

Birth:	BET 1855 AND 1856, Buncombe County, North Carolina[2]
Father:	**Elijah MORGAN** (9 Aug 1824-27 Oct 1879)
Mother:	**Jane GREEN** (11 Sep 1828-18 Jan 1890)

1.1.11.5 Richard Cansler MORGAN[5,2]

Birth:	BET 1857 AND 1858, Buncombe County, North Carolina[2]
Father:	**Elijah MORGAN** (9 Aug 1824-27 Oct 1879)
Mother:	**Jane GREEN** (11 Sep 1828-18 Jan 1890)
Spouse:	**Mattie L. COLE** (BET 1858 AND 1859-)
Birth:	BET 1858 AND 1859, Buncombe County, North Carolina[2]
Marriage:	25 Mar 1881, Buncombe County, North Carolina[5,3]

1.1.11.6 Laura J. MORGAN[5,2]

Birth:	abt 1859, Buncombe County, North Carolina[2]
Father:	**Elijah MORGAN** (9 Aug 1824-27 Oct 1879)
Mother:	**Jane GREEN** (11 Sep 1828-18 Jan 1890)

1.1.11.7 George L. MORGAN[5,2]

Birth:	BET 1860 AND 1861, Buncombe County, North Carolina[2]
Father:	**Elijah MORGAN** (9 Aug 1824-27 Oct 1879)
Mother:	**Jane GREEN** (11 Sep 1828-18 Jan 1890)

1.1.11.8 Bilton MORGAN[5,2]

Birth:	BET 1862 AND 1863, Buncombe County, North Carolina[2]
Father:	**Elijah MORGAN** (9 Aug 1824-27 Oct 1879)
Mother:	**Jane GREEN** (11 Sep 1828-18 Jan 1890)

1.1.11.9 Texas E. MORGAN[5,2]

Birth:	BET 1866 AND 1867, Buncombe County, North Carolina[2]
Father:	**Elijah MORGAN** (9 Aug 1824-27 Oct 1879)
Mother:	**Jane GREEN** (11 Sep 1828-18 Jan 1890)
Spouse:	**A. Z. WRIGHT** (BET 1866 AND 1867-)
Birth:	BET 1866 AND 1867, Buncombe County, North Carolina[2]
Marriage:	24 Feb 1887, Buncombe County, North Carolina[5,3]

1.1.11.10 Etta MORGAN[5,2]

Birth:	BET 1874 AND 1875, Buncombe County, North Carolina[2]
Father:	**Elijah MORGAN** (9 Aug 1824-27 Oct 1879)
Mother:	**Jane GREEN** (11 Sep 1828-18 Jan 1890)
Spouse:	**R. F. LINDSEY** (BET 1870 AND 1871-)
Birth:	BET 1870 AND 1871, Buncombe County, North Carolina[2]
Marriage:	5 Jun 1895, Buncombe County, North Carolina[5,3]

1.1.12 Stephen A. MORGAN Sr.[1,2]

Birth:	BET 1827 AND 1828, Buncombe County, North Carolina[2]
Death:	aft 1880, Buncombe County, North Carolina[2]
Father:	**James Squire MORGAN** (27 Oct 1780-25 Oct 1854)
Mother:	**Margaret (Peggy) GRANT** (abt 1788-10 Sep 1845)

Spouse: **Mary MORGAN** (BET 1834 AND 1835-)
Birth: BET 1834 AND 1835, Buncombe County, North Carolina[2]
Marriage: BET 1850 AND 1856, Buncombe County, North Carolina[3]

7 Children...
      Rebecca C. (BET 1854 AND 1855-)
      James C. (BET 1855 AND 1856-)
      Jasper (BET 1859 AND 1860-)
      Stephen A. Jr. (abt 1860-)
      Margaret (BET 1861 AND 1862-)
      Mary A. (BET 1864 AND 1865-)
      Jethro (BET 1869 AND 1870-)

1.1.12.1 Rebecca C. MORGAN[5,2]

Birth: BET 1854 AND 1855, Buncombe County, North Carolina[2]
Father: **Stephen A. MORGAN Sr.** (BET 1827 AND 1828-aft 1880)
Mother: **Mary MORGAN** (BET 1834 AND 1835-)

Spouse: **Charles H. JAMISON** (BET 1855 AND 1856-)
Birth: BET 1855 AND 1856, Buncombe County, North Carolina[2]
Marriage: 3 Mar 1878, Buncombe County, North Carolina[5,3]

1.1.12.2 James C. MORGAN[5,2]

Birth: BET 1855 AND 1856, Buncombe County, North Carolina[2]
Father: **Stephen A. MORGAN Sr.** (BET 1827 AND 1828-aft 1880)
Mother: **Mary MORGAN** (BET 1834 AND 1835-)

Spouse: **May A. DAVIS** (BET 1858 AND 1859-)
Birth: BET 1858 AND 1859, Buncombe County, North Carolina[2]
Marriage: 11 Sep 1881, Buncombe County, North Carolina[5,3]

1.1.12.3 Jasper MORGAN[5,2]

Birth: BET 1859 AND 1860, Buncombe County, North Carolina[2]
Father: **Stephen A. MORGAN Sr.** (BET 1827 AND 1828-aft 1880)
Mother: **Mary MORGAN** (BET 1834 AND 1835-)

1.1.12.4 Stephen A. MORGAN Jr.[5,2]

Birth: abt 1860, Buncombe County, North Carolina[2]

Father: **Stephen A. MORGAN Sr.** (BET 1827 AND 1828-aft 1880)
Mother: **Mary MORGAN** (BET 1834 AND 1835-)

Spouse: **Hester SMATHERS** (BET 1863 AND 1864-)
Birth: BET 1863 AND 1864, Buncombe County, North Carolina[2]
Marriage: 27 Feb 1882, Buncombe County, North Carolina[5,3]

1.1.12.5 Margaret MORGAN[5,2]

Birth: BET 1861 AND 1862, Buncombe County, North Carolina[2]
Father: **Stephen A. MORGAN Sr.** (BET 1827 AND 1828-aft 1880)
Mother: **Mary MORGAN** (BET 1834 AND 1835-)

1.1.12.6 Mary A. MORGAN[5,2]

Birth: BET 1864 AND 1865, Buncombe County, North Carolina[2]
Father: **Stephen A. MORGAN Sr.** (BET 1827 AND 1828-aft 1880)
Mother: **Mary MORGAN** (BET 1834 AND 1835-)

1.1.12.7 Jethro MORGAN[5,2]

Birth: BET 1869 AND 1870, Buncombe County, North Carolina[2]
Father: **Stephen A. MORGAN Sr.** (BET 1827 AND 1828-aft 1880)
Mother: **Mary MORGAN** (BET 1834 AND 1835-)

1.1.13 John Gano MORGAN[1,2]

Birth: BET 1828 AND 1829, Buncombe County, North Carolina[2]
Death: aft 1880, Buncombe County, North Carolina[2]
Father: **James Squire MORGAN** (27 Oct 1780-25 Oct 1854)
Mother: **Margaret (Peggy) GRANT** (abt 1788-10 Sep 1845)

Spouse: **S. Jane PEEBLES** (BET 1835 AND 1836-aft 1880)
Birth: BET 1835 AND 1836, Buncombe County, North Carolina[2]
Death: aft 1880, Buncombe County, North Carolina[2]
Marriage: 16 Dec 1860, Buncombe County, North Carolina[5,3]

11 Children...
    George (BET 1860 AND 1861-)
    John D. (BET 1861 AND 1862-)
    James Pinkney (BET 1865 AND 1866-)
    Rachel (BET 1866 AND 1867-)
    Margaret (BET 1868 AND 1869-)

Letha (BET 1869 AND 1870-)
Lenore (BET 1870 AND 1871-)
Zeb (BET 1873 AND 1874-)
Caroline (BET 1874 AND 1875-)
Russell Elijah (BET 1876 AND 1877-)
James L. (abt Feb 1880-)

1.1.13.1 George MORGAN[5,2]

Birth:	BET 1860 AND 1861, Buncombe County, North Carolina[2]
Father:	**John Gano MORGAN** (BET 1828 AND 1829-aft 1880)
Mother:	**S. Jane PEEBLES** (BET 1835 AND 1836-aft 1880)

1.1.13.2 John D. MORGAN[6,2]

Birth:	BET 1861 AND 1862, Buncombe County, North Carolina[2]
Father:	**John Gano MORGAN** (BET 1828 AND 1829-aft 1880)
Mother:	**S. Jane PEEBLES** (BET 1835 AND 1836-aft 1880)

1.1.13.3 James Pinkney MORGAN[5,2]

Birth:	BET 1865 AND 1866, Buncombe County, North Carolina[2]
Father:	**John Gano MORGAN** (BET 1828 AND 1829-aft 1880)
Mother:	**S. Jane PEEBLES** (BET 1835 AND 1836-aft 1880)

1.1.13.4 Rachel MORGAN[5,2]

Birth:	BET 1866 AND 1867, Buncombe County, North Carolina[2]
Father:	**John Gano MORGAN** (BET 1828 AND 1829-aft 1880)
Mother:	**S. Jane PEEBLES** (BET 1835 AND 1836-aft 1880)

1.1.13.5 Margaret MORGAN[5,2]

Birth:	BET 1868 AND 1869, Buncombe County, North Carolina[2]
Father:	**John Gano MORGAN** (BET 1828 AND 1829-aft 1880)
Mother:	**S. Jane PEEBLES** (BET 1835 AND 1836-aft 1880)

1.1.13.6 Letha MORGAN[5,2]

Birth:	BET 1869 AND 1870, Buncombe County, North Carolina[2]
Father:	**John Gano MORGAN** (BET 1828 AND 1829-aft 1880)
Mother:	**S. Jane PEEBLES** (BET 1835 AND 1836-aft 1880)

1.1.13.7 Lenore MORGAN[5,2]

Birth:	BET 1870 AND 1871, Buncombe County, North Carolina[2]
Father:	**John Gano MORGAN** (BET 1828 AND 1829-aft 1880)
Mother:	**S. Jane PEEBLES** (BET 1835 AND 1836-aft 1880)

1.1.13.8 Zeb MORGAN[5,2]

Birth:	BET 1873 AND 1874, Buncombe County, North Carolina[2]
Father:	**John Gano MORGAN** (BET 1828 AND 1829-aft 1880)
Mother:	**S. Jane PEEBLES** (BET 1835 AND 1836-aft 1880)

1.1.13.9 Caroline MORGAN[5,2]

Birth:	BET 1874 AND 1875, Buncombe County, North Carolina[2]
Father:	**John Gano MORGAN** (BET 1828 AND 1829-aft 1880)
Mother:	**S. Jane PEEBLES** (BET 1835 AND 1836-aft 1880)

1.1.13.10 Russell Elijah MORGAN[5,2]

Birth:	BET 1876 AND 1877, Buncombe County, North Carolina[2]
Father:	**John Gano MORGAN** (BET 1828 AND 1829-aft 1880)
Mother:	**S. Jane PEEBLES** (BET 1835 AND 1836-aft 1880)

1.1.13.11 James L. MORGAN[5,2]

Birth:	abt Feb 1880, Buncombe County, North Carolina[2]
Father:	**John Gano MORGAN** (BET 1828 AND 1829-aft 1880)
Mother:	**S. Jane PEEBLES** (BET 1835 AND 1836-aft 1880)

1.1.14 Martha MORGAN[1,2]

Birth:	BET 1839 AND 1840, Buncombe County, North Carolina[2]
Father:	**James Squire MORGAN** (27 Oct 1780-25 Oct 1854)
Mother:	**Margaret (Peggy) GRANT** (abt 1788-10 Sep 1845)

Spouse:	**John P. MORGAN** (BET 1837 AND 1838-abt 1915)
Birth:	BET 1837 AND 1838, Buncombe County, North Carolina[2]
Death:	abt 1915[2]
Father:	**Jesse MORGAN** (BET 1780 AND 1824-)
Mother:	**Ann JUSTICE** (BET 1800 AND 1824-)

SOURCES

1. Marty Grant, Web Page (www.martygrant.com) Alton Phillips Rd., Kinston, NC www.martygrant.com/gen/grant/grant-gen.htm, Marty Grants Genealogy Pages, 28504-8614, marty@martygrant.com (family member).
http://www.martygrant.com/gen/grant/grant-gen.htm, Marty Grants Genealogy Pages.
2. Family Members, Hensley, Monroe County, TN. Date of Import: Feb 14, 1999.
3. Family Members, Hensley, Monroe County, TN. Date of Import: Nov 4, 1998.
4. Marty Grant, Web Page (www.martygrant.com) Alton Phillips Rd., Kinston, NC www.martygrant.com/gen/grant/grant-gen.htm, Marty Grants Genealogy Pages, 28504-8614, marty@martygrant.com (family member).
http://www.martygrant.com/gen/grant/grant-gen.htm.
5. Marty Grant, Web Page (www.martygrant.com) Alton Phillips Rd., Kinston, NC www.martygrant.com/gen/grant/grant-gen.htm, Marty Grants Genealogy Pages, 28504-8614, marty@martygrant.com (family member).
http://www.martygrant.com/gen/grant/grant-gen.htm, Marty Grants Genealogy Pages.
6. Marty Grant, Web Page (www.martygrant.com) Alton Phillips Rd., Kinston, NC www.martygrant.com/gen/grant/grant-gen.htm, Marty Grants Genealogy Pages, 28504-8614, marty@martygrant.com (family member).
http://www.martygrant.com/gen/grant/grant-gen.htm, Marty Grants Genealogy Pages.

ADDITIONAL SOURCES

- http://www.genealogy.com/forum/surnames/topics/morgan/1280/
- https://www.findagrave.com/memorial/14905063/perminter-morgan
- http://www.martygrant.com/genealogy/familydata/grpf2205.html
- http://highlandhomepage.danmohn.net/family.php?id=F92143&main_person=I 247633
- https://www.findagrave.com/memorial/15171252/permenter-morgan

INDEX

James	1.1.6.4
Margaret	1.1.6.3
Mary	1.1.6.7
Permenter	1.1.6.2
Pinkney	1.1.6.5
Sarah	1.1.6.1
William	spouse of 1.1.6

JAMISON

Charles H.	spouse of 1.1.12.1

JONES

Gracie	spouse of 1
Vicie (Vickie?)	spouse of 1.1.7.10
W. M.	spouse of 1.1.7.8
William Edward	spouse of 1.1.2.6

JOYCE

Nancy	spouse of 1.1.2.2

JUSTICE

Ann	parent of spouse of 1.1.14

LINDSEY

R. F.	spouse of 1.1.11.10

LUTHER

John	spouse of 1.1.2.5

McCLURE

Emiline	spouse of 1.1.4b.1

MILLER

Henry H.	parent of spouse of 1.1.7.6
Jeptha Irenious	spouse of 1.1.7.3
Margaret M.	spouse of 1.1.7.5
Mary (Polly) A.	spouse of 1.1.7.6

MORGAN

Bilton	1.1.11.8
Carolina	1.1.5.1
Caroline	1.1.13.9
Charity	1.1.2.6
Columbus M.	1.1.11.4
Elijah	1.1.11
Elijah	1.1.4b.2
Elisha Wilson	1.1.2.1
Elizabeth	1.1.7.11
Elizabeth	1.1.4b.4
Elmira	spouse of 1.1.5.2.1
Enoch	1.1.4a.6
Enoch J.	1.1.7.9

Etta	1.1.11.10
George	1.1.13.1
George L.	1.1.11.7
George W.	1.1.9.2
Grace	spouse of 1.1.7
James	1.1.9
James	1.1.7.2
James	1.1.4a.5
James C.	1.1.12.2
James L.	1.1.13.11
James M.	1.1.2.2
James Pinkney	1.1.13.3
James Squire	1.1
James Wilson	1.1.11.1
Jasper	1.1.12.3
Jefferson L.	1.1.4b.3a
Jeremiah	1.1.11.2
Jesse	parent of spouse of 1.1.14
Jesse	parent of spouse of 1.1.4a
Jethro	1.1.12.7
John D.	1.1.13.2
John Gano	1.1.13
John P.	spouse of 1.1.14
Jonathan	1.1.4a.2
Jonathan L.	1.1.5.3
Jonathon	parent of spouse of 1.1.7
Jones H.	1.1.5
Jones H.	1.1.5.5
Laura J.	1.1.11.6
Lavada	1.1.2.8
Lenore	1.1.13.7
Letha	1.1.13.6
Lewis R.	1.1.7
Lewis Webster	1.1.7.5
Lucinda	1.1.4a.8
Margaret	1.1.6
Margaret	1.1.4a.4
Margaret	1.1.2.5
Margaret	1.1.9.3
Margaret	1.1.12.5
Margaret	1.1.13.5
Margaret L.	1.1.7.3
Margaret (Peggy)	spouse of 1.1.4a

Marion	1.1.5.7
Martha	1.1.8
Martha	1.1.4a.3
Martha	1.1.14
Martha	1.1.9.4
Martha	1.1.7.12
Martha E.	1.1.5.6
Mary	spouse of 1.1.12
Mary	1.1.4a.7
Mary A.	1.1.12.6
Mary C.	1.1.7.8
Mary J.	1.1.9.1
Mary (Polly)	1.1.3
Mary (Polly) Ann	spouse of 1.1.7.9
Millie	1.1.10
Morris Grant Sr.	1.1.4a
Morris Grant Jr.	1.1.4a.9
Moses S.	1.1.7.7
Noah	1.1.7.10
Permenter	1
Permenter D. Sr.	1.1.2
Permenter D. Jr.	1.1.2.4
Permenter S.	1.1.7.6
Pinkney	1.1.7.4
Rachel	1.1.13.4
Rebecca	1.1.4a.1
Rebecca	1.1.7.1
Rebecca	1.1.5.2.2
Rebecca A.	1.1.5.2
Rebecca C.	1.1.12.1
Richard Cansler	1.1.11.5
Russell Elijah	1.1.13.10
Silas Lafayette	1.1.5.2.1
Silas M.	spouse of 1.1.5.2
Stacy	1.1.2.7
Stephen A. Sr.	1.1.12
Stephen A. Jr.	1.1.12.4
Susan Tabitha	1.1.1
Texas E.	1.1.11.9
Thomas	1.1.7.13
Tilitha	1.1.11.3
William	1.1.2.3
William Permenter	1.1.4b.1

Wilson	1.1.5.4
Zeb	1.1.13.8
MORRIS	
Susanna	parent of spouse of 1.1
NEAL	
Julia	spouse of 1.1.8.5
NICHOLS	
Daniel	spouse of 1.1.4b.4
OWENBY	
Rachel	spouse of 1.1.4a.9
PARKER	
Robert H.	spouse of 1.1.4a.1
PEEBLES	
Mary Ann	spouse of 1.1.8.6
S. Jane	spouse of 1.1.13
William	spouse of 1.1.4a.3
SAWYER	
Caroline	spouse of 1.1.9.2
SMATHERS	
Hester	spouse of 1.1.12.4
Nancy	spouse of 1.1.2.1
TAYLOR	
Elizabeth	spouse of 1.1.4a
THOMPSON	
Reverend James	spouse of 1.1.10
Mary E.	spouse of 1.1.7.7
THRASH	
J. Lee	spouse of 1.1.2.8
WARREN	
Elberry	1.1.8.6
Hannah Amanda	spouse of 1.1.9
James	parent of spouse of 1.1.1
James	1.1.8.3
Joseph	spouse of 1.1.1.2
Josiah	1.1.1.3
Margaret	1.1.8.2
Mary S.	1.1.1.1
Milly L.	1.1.1.2
Naomi	1.1.8.1
R. Morris	1.1.8.5
Rachel	parent of spouse of 1.1.7.6
Robert	spouse of 1.1.8
Uriah Sr.	spouse of 1.1.1

Uriah Jr.   1.1.1.4
William H.   1.1.1.5
William Lafayette   1.1.8.4

WIFE OF JAMES WARREN
UNNAMED   parent of spouse of 1.1.1

WIFE OF JONATHON L. MORGAN
Jane   spouse of 1.1.5.3

WIFE OF JONES H. MORGAN
Mary L.   spouse of 1.1.5.5

WILKERSON
Rebecca   parent of spouse of 1.1.7

WRIGHT
A. Z.   spouse of 1.1.11.9
N. M.   spouse of 1.1.1.5

YOUNG
Charity   spouse of 1.1.2
Rebecca   spouse of 1.1.5
Rebecca   spouse of 1.1.2.3

NOTES

NOTES

NOTES

Family Lineage of Permenter Morgan and Descendants of Rutherford and Buncombe. North Carolina (2018 Edition)

Page 41 of 46

NOTES

ABOUT THE AUTHOR

Dawn D. Boyer, Ph.D.'s journey into the practice of genealogy studies started in her teens when she sat at her paternal grandfather's knee to learn about family members and ancestors as part of a school project. The hobby intensified when she found family history artifacts hidden away in file cabinets while she was working at one employer, and she decided to further research her bosses' fascinating family history and genealogy. The result of her research was a database of over 136,600 names, including her own family history, her bosses' fascinating family history, and the lineage of Sir John Rolfe and Pocahontas. She has taken the data researched over the last 20+ years and compiled family histories and lineages for more than 300 unique surnames in her database.

She is the author of 270+ books on the topics of genealogy, family lineage, adult education and androgogy women and gender studies, business- and career-search practices, memoirs, quotes for self-improvement and motivation (2,000+ / 3,000+ series), and her 'Interview with an Artist' series (three artists in the series to date), as well as over 75 adult coloring books.

She completed her Doctor of Philosophy in Education (Occupational & Technical Studies, with a concentration in Training & Development in Human Resources) from Old Dominion University in Norfolk, VA in 2013. Her dissertation is entitled, 'Competencies of Human Resources Practitioners within the Government Contracting Industry,' which identified unique KSAs for Human Resources Managers working for federal level government contracting companies. This groundbreaking research was the impetus upon her textbook guide for Human Resources Professionals in Government Contracting, completed in 2017 and for sale on Amazon.

She has been an entrepreneur and business owner for 20+ years, currently in her consulting firm, D. Boyer Consulting, based in Richmond (Henrico County), VA, and servicing clients internationally. Her background experience is 24+ years in the Human Resources field, of which 11 years are within the federal defense contracting industry. Dr. Boyer's experience in federal (defense) contracting as a Human Resources Director or Senior Manager has provided her insight, experience, practice, and capabilities to perform within this industry, as well as instruct others to abilities needed in middle-management or executive human resource roles.

Dr. Boyer manages her own business offering job seekers Search Engine Optimized (SEO) resumes for increased visibility to recruiters – getting the candidates past the recruiting 'firewall' and connected for interviews for faster hires and job placement. Her tech-based knowledge of how ATS software systems work allows her to structure resumes for recruiters' Boolean search queries. Her SEO coding within resumes is so unique, no other resume writers offer this service.

She assists (23 authors as of this publication date) academics and writers publish their works or manuscripts as a third-party publisher – DBC Publishing. She also assists business owners develop their brand and marketing plans within social media marketing, planning, and management and as a mentor through the Small Business Administraiton's Senior Corps of Retired Executives (now simply referred to as SCORE).

Dr. Boyer is active on social media and invites readers to connect to her on these platforms:

All of Dr. Boyer's books are listed on her Amazon author's page at:

https: //www.amazon.com/author/dawnboyer.

She May be reached via her business website:

http: //DBoyerConsulting.com

or by email:

Dawn.Boyer@DBoyerConsulting.com

Interested in publishing your own academic essays, projects, or books?
Contact the author for publishing project estimates, consulting, and assistance:

Dawn.Boyer@me.com

www.DBoyerConsulting.com

Follow the Author on Social Media Platforms

D. Boyer Consulting / DBoyerConsulting.com

Join her 13,000+ connections on LinkedIn:
www.linkedin.com/in/DawnBoyer

Amazon Author Page:
www.amazon.com/author/dawnboyer

Review Author's books:
www.shelfari.com/DawnDeniseBoyer

Follow her on Twitter at:
www.Twitter.com/Dawn_Boyer

Subscribe to her YouTube Channel:
www.youtube.com/user/DawnDeniseBoyer

ABOUT THE BOOK

The **Family Lineage of Permenter Morgan and Descendants of Rutherford and Buncombe, North Carolina** provides a lineage of **Permenter Morgan** who was born between **1730 and 1765**, down through history to more modern-day descendants who were born as recently as the 1900's and living predominately in **Rutherford and Buncombe, North Carolina**. This book provides at least four (4) generations of direct descendants and their spouses.

If you are a serious or hobby genealogist, and researching the **Morgan** lineage, this book could provide you some lineage data and vital statistics information you have been seeking to link your family or surname to this line of **Morgans**.

Included in this lineage's volume are source notes from which the data was collected and an index of names.

Made in the USA
Las Vegas, NV
21 January 2022